KU-266-664

TERRORISM

© Aladdin Books Ltd

*First published in
Great Britain in 1986 by*
Franklin Watts
12a Golden Square
London W1

Designed and produced by
Aladdin Books Ltd
70 Old Compton Street
London W1

ISBN 086313 393 2

The front cover photograph shows a terrorist incident in the streets of Beirut, Lebanon. The back cover photograph shows a political mural in Belfast, Northern Ireland.

The author, Dr Christopher Coker, is a lecturer in International Relations at the London School of Economics, London, UK.

The consultant, Dr John Pimlott, is Senior Lecturer in the Department of War Studies and International Affairs, RMA, Sandhurst, UK.

Contents

S...ISSUES...ISSU

TERRORISM

CHRISTOPHER COKER

Illustrated by
Ron Hayward Associates

Franklin Watts
London : New York : Toronto : Sydney

Introduction

Every month we can read of outrages committed around the world: 150 holidaymakers taken hostage on a cruise liner in the Mediterranean; an aircraft hijacked in Beirut; a bomb explodes in an attempt to blow up the entire British government. These events are examples of *political violence*: they are acts of terrorism.

Terrorist organisations use terror *itself* as a device to create fear and panic, and not simply in a government or just a social group, but in the whole population. Their actions are criminal and may seem random, but they are not mindless.

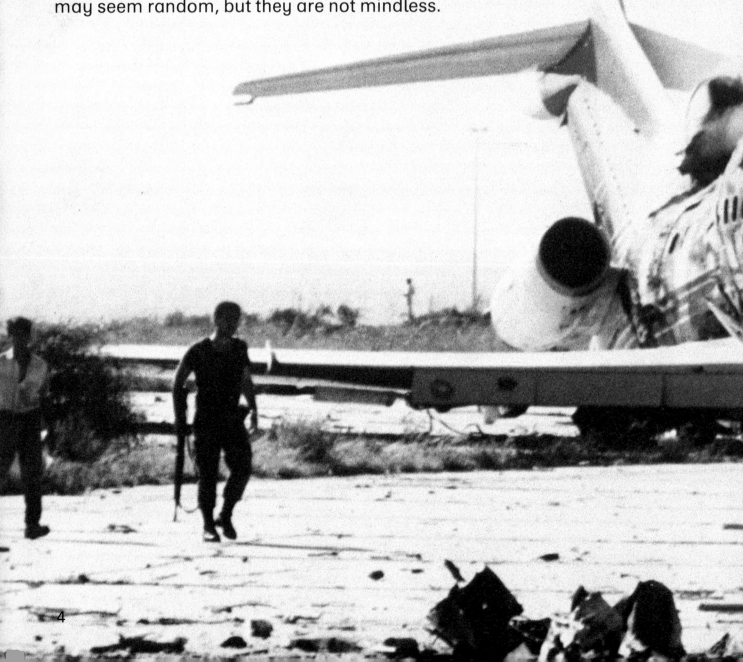

▽ Beirut airport, Lebanon, June 1985: a hijacked Jordanian aircraft burns after being blown up by Muslim terrorists. Disturbing evidence of the growth of terrorism, such sights have become quite frequent in certain parts of the world.

By selecting specific targets, such as aircraft, shops or stations, terrorists want to show that the state cannot protect its citizens. By doing so, they hope to create a climate of fear which makes it impossible for life to function normally.

Yet world governments are not co-ordinated to deal with the problem: one man's terrorist is another man's freedom fighter. As long as the world is unable to agree on a common definition of terrorism, it is unlikely to act decisively against it. As a result, terrorism is growing and has become one of today's most frightening problems.

Escalation

Terrorism is not new – the first historically recognised terrorist incidents occurred in the 19th century – but it has grown dramatically in the last 20 years. Since the 1970s, the world has seen an alarming growth in the number of terrorist movements and in the actual methods they use.

This increase has been partly due to the fact that terrorists now help each other, but more significantly, to international publicity. Television coverage has enabled terrorist ideas to travel from country to country, producing new organisations. For example, in the USA, the Black Panthers produced the White Panthers, and the Tupamaros in Uruguay inspired the creation of the Tupamaros West Berlin.

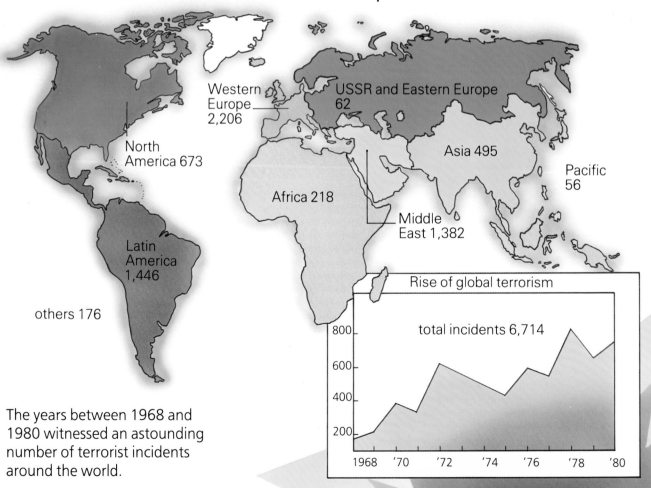

Western Europe 2,206

USSR and Eastern Europe 62

North America 673

Asia 495

Africa 218

Pacific 56

Latin America 1,446

Middle East 1,382

others 176

Rise of global terrorism

total incidents 6,714

800
600
400
200

1968 '70 '72 '74 '76 '78 '80

The years between 1968 and 1980 witnessed an astounding number of terrorist incidents around the world.

Major terrorist attacks in Europe in 1975

Sweden 2

Northern Ireland

Britain

Eire 5

4

6 Netherlands

1

West Germany

France

7 Austria

Italy

Yugoslavia

Spain 3

International publicity has also led terrorist groups to copy each other's methods, so that along with such traditional terrorist practices as assassination and hostage taking, the world is now witnessing more hijacking of aircraft and embassy sieges. The hijacking of American aircraft to Cuba, for example, was imitated around the world, reaching a peak of 82 such incidents in 1969. The kidnapping of the US ambassador in Brazil, in September 1969, was copied by so many groups, that between 1969-75 there was an attempted kidnapping of an American diplomat once every three months, and a successful kidnapping once every five!

Both in its scale and scope, the world had seen nothing like this kind of terrorist activity before. However we must not exaggerate its impact: it did not bring society to a halt.

△ 1975 was a fairly typical year for terrorist attacks. Among the many incidents in Europe, some of the major examples were: (1) two attempts to shoot down airliners leaving Orly airport (Paris, France); the seizure of embassies in (2) Stockholm (Sweden) and (3) Madrid (Spain); (4) an IRA bombing campaign in London (UK) and (5) the kidnapping of a Dutch businessman in Eire; (6) the hijacking of a train by South Moluccan terrorists in the Netherlands and (7) the kidnapping of Arab oil ministers at a meeting in Vienna (Austria).

Why terrorism?

People who turn to political violence do so for various reasons. In many countries, it is because they find themselves in conflict with unjust, repressive governments, or perhaps because they come from underprivileged social groups.

However, in Western societies this is not the case. A recent study found that 90 per cent of the members of European terrorist movements are intelligent young men and women from wealthy, middle-class families. They become terrorists as a means of *political* expression. They are opposed to capitalist society – a society which places great importance on material values. However, there are other reasons to explain why people turn to terrorism.

The Baader-Meinhof gang
The Baader-Meinhof gang in West Germany, known as the Red Army Faction (RAF), is the classic example of a group of disenchanted young people who turned to terrorism in the early 1970s. Ulrike Meinhof, Andreas Baader and Gudrun Ensslin were founder members of the gang. Trained by the PLO in the Lebanon, the gang carried out a number of embassy sieges and spectacular kidnappings. Hanns-Martin Schleyer (photograph left) was one such victim, kidnapped in 1977 and subsequently murdered. Most of the leaders committed suicide in prison. They were aided by their lawyers who smuggled in the arms.

Elsewhere in the world, people who are part of discontented ethnic groups within a country turn to terrorism for reasons of *nationalism*. They want to establish their own nation and win freedom and independence.

More recently, we have seen the gradual emergence of a new form of terrorism which is *religious*, rather than political or nationalist in inspiration. Throughout the Middle East, Muslim groups have begun to fight for the creation of a society which is less Westernised and closer to their religion. Like the other forms of terrorism, however, it represents the need of many people to find some spiritual purpose in an extremely materialistic age.

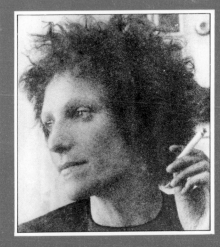

Ulrike Meinhof (1934-76) was the daughter of an art historian and a graduate in philosophy and sociology. In the 1960s, she was a writer for left-wing magazines. She rescued Andreas Baader from prison in 1970. Captured by the police, she committed suicide in 1976.

Andreas Baader (1943-77) was the son of a historian. He was sentenced to three years imprisonment for a bomb attack in Frankfurt at the height of the student unrest in the late 1960s. Rescued in 1970, he established contact with the PLO. He committed suicide with Ensslin in 1977.

Gudrun Ensslin (1940-77) was a clergyman's daughter and a graduate in philosophy and languages. She was sentenced with Baader for the Frankfurt attack. She received training from the PLO. After receiving a life sentence in 1977 for several crimes, she too committed suicide.

Democracy under threat

Democratic countries – where governments genuinely represent the people who elect them – are especially vulnerable to terrorist attacks. One reason for this is that these countries are mostly in the Western, industrialised world, where the complexity of modern society provides many vulnerable targets. Reservoirs can easily be poisoned, electricity grids put out of action, or trains carrying nuclear waste can be derailed.

Democracies are more vulnerable still because the media is not censored. Terrorism *needs* publicity to make its impact, and television, in particular, provides it. Television reports events and is also used to show actual terrorist incidents.

▽ On 20 December 1985, Arab and French terrorists held a court at gunpoint in Nantes, France for over two days. The whole episode was captured on television. Indeed, the terrorists actually *used* the cameras to get their message across to the nation.

The murder of the Israeli athletes at the 1972 Munich Olympic Games was watched by a horrified audience of 500 million people. Television has also been used by terrorists to put over their cases in interviews, and even to show video-taped recordings of victims confessing to alleged "crimes against the people".

Democratic governments are also exposed to terrorism because they tend to be sensitive towards public opinion. Consequently, to ensure that they are not being pushed into extreme measures which would threaten the rights and freedom of their own citizens, they are more likely to show restraint in combating terrorism.

▽ The introduction in the early 1970s of the portable generator, video recorder and lightweight camera, have made it much easier to make "instant news" of terrorist actions. This dramatic example is taken from a television interview with a hijacker at Beirut airport in 1985. The Trans-World airline pilot, John Testrake, displayed remarkable courage throughout his ordeal.

Capitalist societies

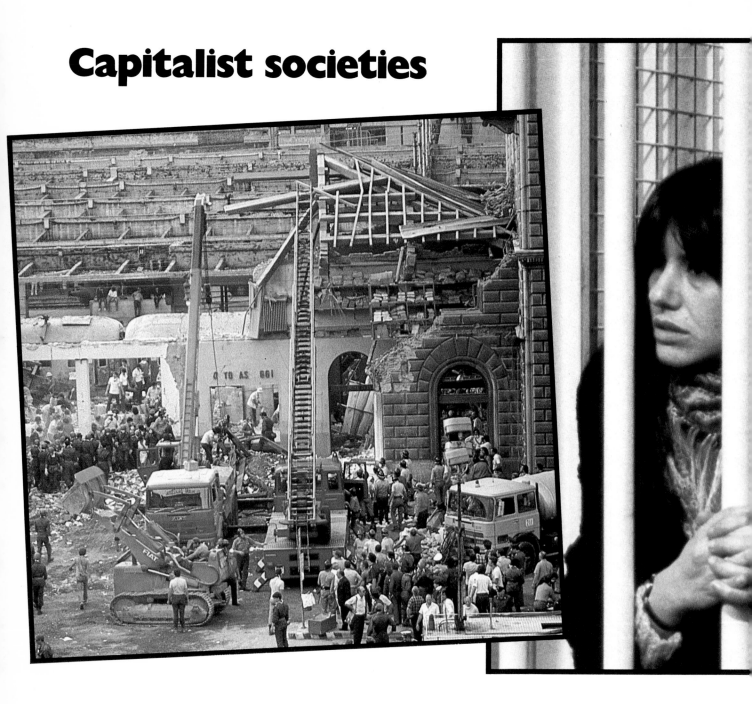

△ The destruction of public centres is one of the most indiscriminate forms of terrorist action. A dramatic example was the bombing of Bologna Station, Italy, in 1980. This outrage is generally believed to have been carried out by *right-wing* terrorists. Although fewer in number than left-wing organisations, right-wing terrorist groups are nevertheless as ruthless in their use of violence.

Modern capitalist societies in North America and Western Europe have produced by far the most extreme terrorist movements. These organisations aim at the destruction of capitalist society. In the USA, for example, a terrorist group called the Weathermen set out to destroy the capitalist system, attacking banks and companies. In 15 months they used no less than 4,300 incendiary bombs.

The members of such organisations usually come from prosperous, middle-class homes.

Nevertheless, they identify with the "exploited" working class. Some groups, like the Red Brigade in Italy, hold politicians and bankers in "people's prisons", where they are tried and often "executed" for crimes against the working class.

However, these groups have found little support. Their actions have been condemned by socialist parties and trade unions. Such terrorist groups are protesting against a lifestyle and living standards which the working classes worked hard to have a share in.

△ The Red Brigade, two members of which are photographed above in prison, has tried to bring down capitalism in Italy. It has been responsible for attacks on factories and communications, and the murder of former Prime Minister Aldo Moro. Moro was forced to admit to "crimes against the people", in a video message to the nation.

Ireland and the IRA

The chart shows:
- 21,200 — troop levels (1972)
- 12,481 — terrorist incidents (1972)
- 13,452 — troop levels (1978)
- 1,503 — terrorist incidents (1978)
- 9,090 — troop levels (1984)
- 592 — terrorist incidents (1984)

troop levels

terrorist incidents

1972   1978   1984

△ In terms of terrorist incidents and troop levels, the situation in Northern Ireland has improved since 1972.

The Irish Republican Army (IRA) has been campaigning to unify Ireland since 1922. Far from seeing itself as a terrorist organisation, it claims it is fighting a war against an occupying force – the British. It hopes the British government will eventually respond to the sheer cost of maintaining order in Northern Ireland – both in terms of lives and money – by pulling out.

So in order to increase the running costs of Northern Ireland's union with Britain, the IRA began a successful campaign, in 1969, to bring down the regional government of Northern Ireland and force the British government to impose direct rule. As part of its aim to increase the cost in human lives, it has continued to attack the British army that was sent in 1969 as a peace-keeping force.

14

THE � TIMES

SATURDAY OCTOBER 13 1984

20p

No 61,961

Conference hotel blast leaves 3 dead, 32 injured and one missing

Thatcher defies IRA bombers

Tories' ovation full of affection

Terrorism will never destroy democracy, the Prime Minister told the final day of the Conservative Party Conference in Brighton yesterday.

Party representatives gave her a long ovation, full of affection and relief at her escape from the bomb blast at her hotel.

Mrs Thatcher was moved, our Political Editor writes, by the warmth of sympathy in the messages she received from Mr Neil Kinnock and other party leaders. **Page 4**

Hotel's strength resisted blast

Police have banned the release of plans of the Grand Hotel, a nine-storey Victorian building first opened in 1864, which was taken over recently by a Warrington company as part of a £44.5m deal.

The blast appears to have been contained by the strong walls of the hotel, described at its opening as a "Cyclopean pile". **Page 3**

Buried under the rubble

"I was sound asleep. I felt a tremendous noise and crashing. I thought it was an earthquake. I was in rubble up to my neck. I kept on wondering how long the air would last. I prayed . . ." That was Mr Harvey Thomas, Conservative conference organizer, David Tytler pieces together events during a night of terror **Page 2**

Autumn bomb campaign fear

The Brighton bombing might signal a Provisional IRA bombing campaign in mainland Britain this autumn. The IRA and Sinn Fein have badly needed a propaganda coup after a series of setbacks including the recent seizure of tons of arms off the coast of co Kerry.

The caller who claimed IRA responsibility for the blast said it was directed at "the British Cabinet and Tory warmongers". **Page 2**

Joseph sleeps through

Sir Keith Joseph, Secretary of State for Education and Science, slept through the blast in his . . .

Aftermath: The Grand Hotel, rent by the bomb blast, photographed 15 minutes after the explosion by John Manning

Tebbit and Chief Whip hurt

Inquiry on security

Questions for the inquiry
● Why were there . . .
on people . . .

Gap still wide in pit talks

By Paul Routledge
Labour Editor

The search for peace in the coal industry will be resumed this afternoon despite strongly-held views on both sides that there is no scope for a settlement of the conflict over colliery closures.

Leaders of the National Union of Mineworkers are going back into talks with the National Coal Board, with a new proposal on the table from the independent Advisory, Conciliation and Arbitration Service (Acas).

The latest peace package has already been given the go-ahead by the National Coal Board, but it does not have the backing of the striking pitmen.

Mr Pat Lowry, chairman of Acas, said last night that the discussions between the two sides had been adjourned on the basis of separate peace documents tabled by Acas. One of these is acceptable to the mineworkers, and the other is acceptable to the National Coal Board.

Acas took delivery late last night of proposals from the miners' union and formulated them into a document which the coal board and the pit deputies' union, Nacods, are considering overnight.

Mr Arthur Scargill, president of the NUM, last night made clear that his union's original demands in the dispute had not changed. The NUM is still demanding the withdrawal of the coal board's March 6 colliery closure programme involving 20 pits and 20,000 jobs.

The coal board's original proposal accepted the idea of an independent advisory body to consider an appeal by any mining union on the prospect of closure at any pit. But its role would be "strictly advisory".

Full weight would be given to the advice tendered by the body, but it would not have a veto on pit shut downs.

A modified suggestion arising from discussions between the parties is being discussed today.

It says that any colliers not agreed to be exhausted either because it has no coal or is unsafe may be brought forward by either party for discussion and investigation in line with Plan for Coal under . . .

△ The IRA bombing of a hotel in Brighton, England, in 1984, was an attempt to assassinate the entire British government, who were attending a conference there. They failed to kill a single senior cabinet member, but four people died and a further 32 were injured.

◁ The IRA views itself as a paramilitary force, the military arm of the Sinn Fein, not a classic terrorist movement. Consequently, IRA members wear military uniforms on parade and fire volleys of ammunition at IRA funerals.

When it became obvious that the British were not going to pull out, the IRA turned its attention to the British people on the mainland with a random bombing campaign. The IRA also resorted to political assassination, from the murder of Lord Mountbatten in 1979, to the attempted assassination of all the key members of the British government in 1984. Alongside these acts of political violence, the movement is now also using its political wing "Sinn Fein" to compete in local and national elections.

The IRA has not succeeded in achieving its main objectives. However, it has succeeded in further dividing the Protestant and Catholic communities. This has made it increasingly difficult for the British government to introduce certain political reforms which might restore the faith of the Catholics in the union with Britain.

16

Palestinian terrorism

◁ In acts of indiscriminate violence, terrorists machine-gunned innocent passengers waiting at El Al check-in desks in Rome and Vienna airports, December 1985.

▽ With the declaration of the state of Israel in 1948, thousands of Palestinians left the country and settled in refugee camps throughout the Middle East. Today their numbers have increased significantly. Inevitably, this has led to friction with local populations. In 1970, the Palestinians were forced out of Jordan and in 1982 they were expelled from the Lebanon by an invading Israeli force.

The Palestinian Liberation Organisation (PLO) was founded in 1964 to campaign for a homeland for the Palestinian people. Convinced it could not rely on its Arab neighbours for help, it turned to political violence to achieve its aims.

However, the PLO has never claimed to be a terrorist movement, but a national liberation movement. In this it has been so successful that in 1974 its chairman, Yasser Arafat, was invited to address the UN General Assembly.

Unfortunately, as the organistion has won such international respectability, it has unwittingly provoked many of its more extreme members to leave and set up independent terrorist organisations. The Popular Democratic Front for the Liberation of Palestine (PDFLP) and the Black September group are two major examples, and a more recent example is Abu Nidal's organisation, responsible for the Rome and Vienna massacres.

other countries 140,000

USA 100,000

Lebanon 347,000

Syria 215,000

Iraq 20,000

Israel

Kuwait 278,000

Libya 23,000

Egypt 48,500

Qatar 22,500

UAE 34,700

Oman 48,200

The Palestinian dispersal 1948-1982

Jordan 1,160,800

Saudi Arabia 127,000

Islamic terrorism

Particularly bewildering to Western observers is a new phenomenon – religious terrorism. Its inspiration was the revolution in Iran in 1978, which brought to power a new government, headed by militant, religious leaders, or "mullahs". Inspired by the Islamic faith, and the promise that martyrs will win a privileged place in heaven, these terrorists have been among the most fanatical of all.

They have built up a complex international network and have begun to forge links with European terrorist organisations, such as the Red Brigade.

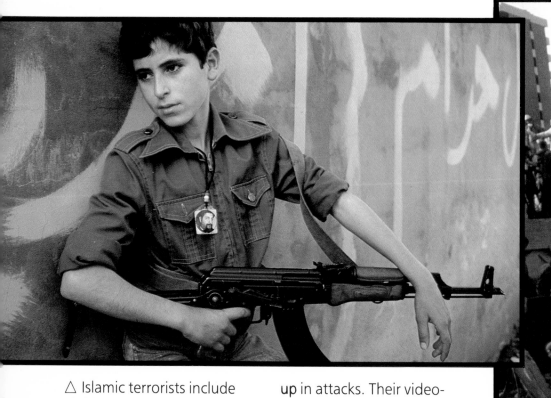

△ Islamic terrorists include children of 15 years old. These children, inspired by religious zeal, have blown themselves up in attacks. Their video-taped messages to the nation were played on Lebanese television after their deaths.

The main battleground for these beliefs is the Lebanon, once the most prosperous and tolerant state in the Middle East, which collapsed into civil war in the mid-1970s. Here terrorists have engaged in a particularly devastating form of violence – car bombings aimed at innocent civilians and embassy compounds.

The most militant group of all, the Islamic Holy War, considers the USA to be the main source of Western influence in the Middle East, and therefore the main threat to Islam. Consequently, in their attacks, US citizens are deliberately singled out.

▽ The two most devastating car bomb attacks were carried out in 1983, against the command posts of the US and French peacekeeping forces in the Lebanon. 241 US servicemen and 58 French soldiers were killed.

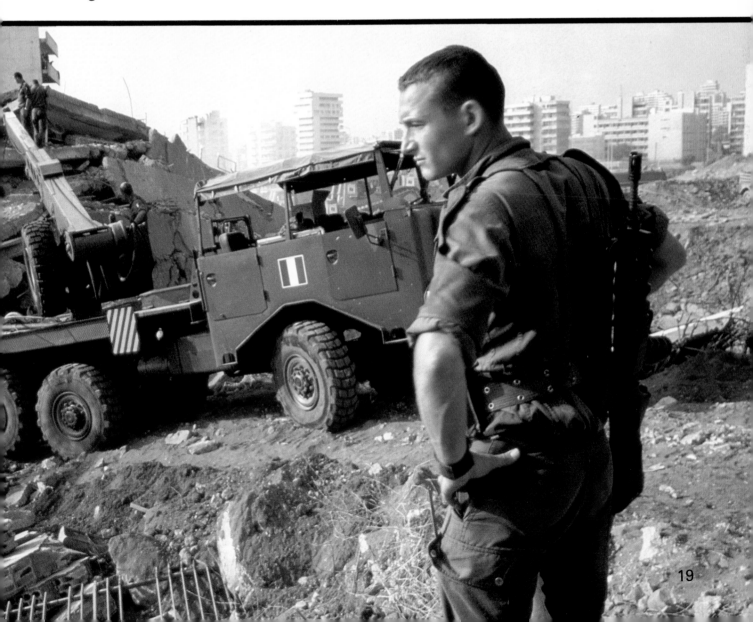

Latin America

The conditions which breed political violence in Latin America are unique. It is one of the poorest regions in the world, where cities have grown faster than anywhere else, creating vast slums.

So it is not surprising that the terrorists' targets have been the symbols of wealth in a land of poverty: landowners, businessmen, and foreign companies, mostly US – all are alleged to exploit the peasants. Through their actions, these terrorist groups hope to make the people aware of their wretched condition and be prepared to act to change it.

▽ In Latin America, terrorists are dealing with often harsh, military governments. These regimes are often prepared to resort to terrorism themselves. In Argentina, the police formed "murder squads", which eliminated over 20,000 suspected terrorist supporters. In Uruguay, the Tupamaros were virtually wiped out, by which time, however, one in ten Uruguayan citizens were in jail.

Here, kidnapping is one of the most commonly used tactics, both for political reasons and because it helps to bring in funds. Such funds enabled one terrorist group, the Tupamaros in Uruguay, to achieve enough publicity and popularity to be able to blackmail companies into distributing free food, and free medical supplies to hospitals.

The kidnapping of businessmen began in 1971, and the present ransom record is a staggering $60 million, paid to the Argentinian group, the "Montoneros", for two hostages in 1974.

▽ The sight of terrorists who have died at the army's hands is a frequent one in many Latin American countries. Often the dead are left where they have been killed, to discourage others from joining terrorist movements. The cans on the back of the truck are actually home-made bombs.

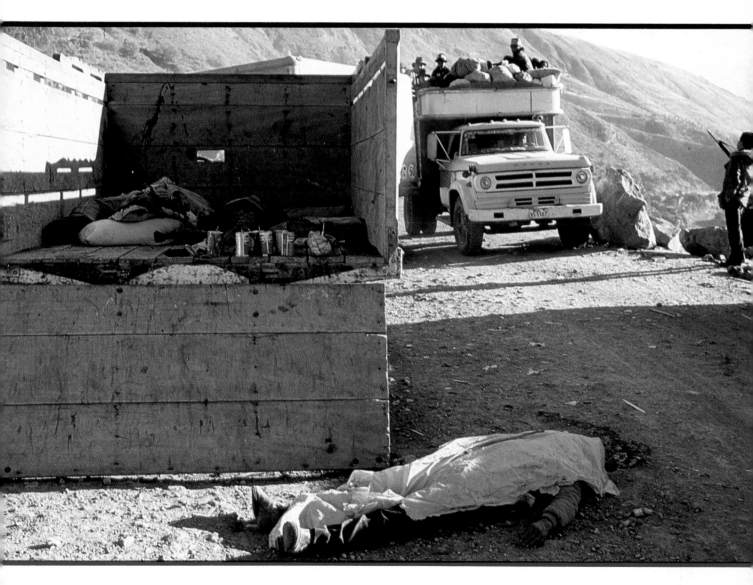

Global links

All terrorists believe in world revolution and so their organisations help each other throughout the world, and involve themselves in each other's causes. They provide each other with forged passports and visas, so that they can travel more easily, and even with arms and training. The PLO, for example, has trained Basque terrorists in the Yemen, the Baader-Meinhof gang in the Lebanon, and also the Black Panthers. It has even trained right-wing, neo-Nazi German groups. Terrorists have also co-operated in actual operations, such as the attack on Lod Airport, Israel, in 1972.

This international network is now extensive and is still growing. However, it makes the groups vulnerable. The links can be broken in any part of the chain – the more information they share, the harder it is to keep secret – and the movements can also be penetrated more easily by the police.

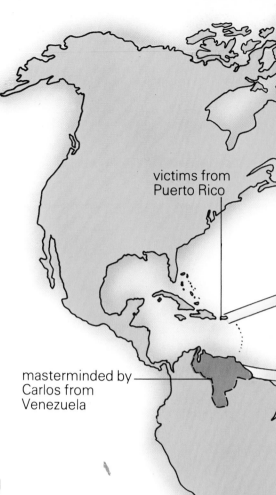

victims from Puerto Rico

masterminded by Carlos from Venezuela

◁ "Carlos" is the name used by a Venezuelan terrorist with extensive international contacts. He trained in Cuba in terrorist tactics in the 1960s, sponsored by the KGB, the Soviet Secret Service. In 1970 he made contact with the leaders of the Baader-Meinhof gang. In 1975 he took over a PLO group operating in Paris. The seizure of Arab oil ministers in Vienna two years later was masterminded by Carlos, aided by the Baader-Meinhof gang. After the Vienna raid, Carlos disappeared from the active terrorist scene in Europe, hunted by the world's police.

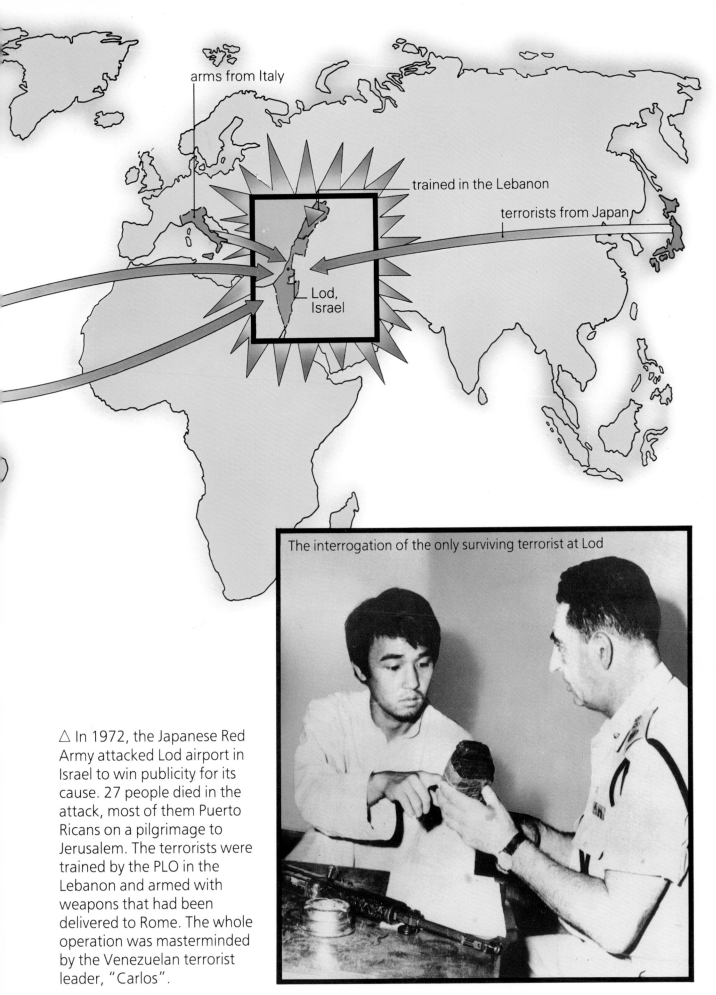

arms from Italy

trained in the Lebanon

terrorists from Japan

Lod, Israel

The interrogation of the only surviving terrorist at Lod

△ In 1972, the Japanese Red Army attacked Lod airport in Israel to win publicity for its cause. 27 people died in the attack, most of them Puerto Ricans on a pilgrimage to Jerusalem. The terrorists were trained by the PLO in the Lebanon and armed with weapons that had been delivered to Rome. The whole operation was masterminded by the Venezuelan terrorist leader, "Carlos".

Anti-terrorist squads

The bungled attempt of the West German police to rescue the Israeli athletes at the Munich Olympics in 1972, ended in the deaths of all the 11 athletes concerned. This fiasco, and the steady growth of terrorism in the 1970s, illustrated the need for world governments to set up special groups to combat terrorism.

Some groups, like the GSG-9 in West Germany, are specialist police units. Others, like the SAS in Britain, are made up of regular army personnel, while others, like squads drawn from the Italian Carabinieri, are paramilitary forces, independent both of the army and the police. Members are carefully selected and specially trained.

△ The badge above sums up the total commitment of the SAS in fighting world terrorism.

▽ Members of anti-terrorist squads take part in rigorous training exercises.

24

▽ Governments have been forced to act so decisively in forming anti-terrorist squads partly because of embassy sieges. Of the 550 terrorist incidents between 1979-81, diplomats and diplomatic property were involved in over 200. The success record in dealing with such incidents has been mixed. However, in the Iranian embassy siege in London, 1980 (photographed below) the SAS succeeded in rescuing diplomats held by Arab terrorists, without the loss of a single hostage.

Training is both physical and psychological. It includes unarmed combat and the use of special weapons, like stun grenades (an SAS speciality). These squads also have to have a knowledge of explosives and marksmanship. Moreover, being prepared for certain situations, such as hijacks, requires specific knowledge, from details of airport equipment to becoming part of a ten-man team of cabin personnel. In addition, all special forces are trained in basic bargaining skills, in the hope of talking terrorists out of difficult situations. This is because rescue missions involving violence are extremely difficult to carry off, and so are only used as a last resort.

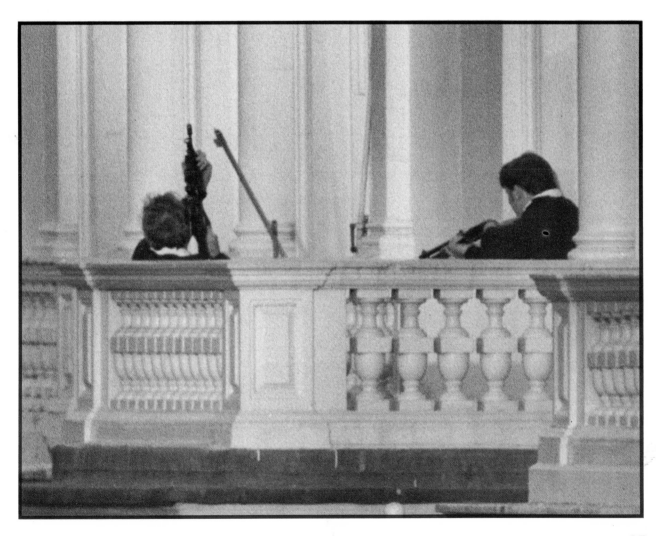

A success story

In 1977, a Lufthansa aircraft was hijacked by Palestinians in support of the Baader-Meinhof gang. The West German anti-terrorist squad, the GSG-9 went into action, aided by two British SAS men. Some 40 minutes before the deadline for the release of the Meinhof gang, 28 German commandos forced the main door of the aircraft, in Mogadishu, Somalia. They killed three of the hijackers outright and rescued the hostages. The whole operation lasted only 11 minutes.

An alternative to force in such situations is negotiation. Many countries try to prolong hostage situations, in the hope of persuading terrorists to give up. At one time it was not unknown for a personal bond to be established between hostages and their captors.

Today, however, to prevent such situations from arising, terrorists have begun to work in small groups, dehumanising their victims by forcing them to remain silent, often blindfolding them, and wearing hoods themselves. As the Mogadishu incident showed when the terrorist leader "executed" the German pilot, terrorists are prepared to kill hostages to break a deadlock in negotiations, or to prove their seriousness.

The Mogadishu rescue

Before the successful outcome of the Mogadishu rescue, many complex manoeuvres took place over several days. On 13 October 1977, the aircraft is hijacked at Palma. After refuelling in Rome and Cyprus, it flies on to the Middle East. At Aden the pilot is shot. It then flies on to Mogadishu, where it lands on 17 October.

Meanwhile, the first of two groups of GSG-9 men leave for Cyprus, but arrive just as the hijacked aircraft takes off. They return to base via Ankara to change aircraft on 15 October, then fly to Crete, and then to Mogadishu. They arrive after dark on 17 October, and at 0150 hours the rescue operation begins. The second group of GSG-9, including West Germany's leading trouble shooter, Hans Jurgen Wischnewski, arrives at Dubai at dawn 15 October. Their Boeing 707 is refused permission to land in Aden and is diverted to Jiddah. It arrives in Mogadishu on 17 October to co-ordinate the rescue operation.

The Mogadishu rescue

✈ The hijackers

✈ GSG-9

✈ Wischnewski

West Germany

Bonn

Frankfurt

Rome

Palma

Crete

Cyprus

Ankara

Turkey

Bahrain

Dubai

Jiddah

Saudi Arabia

South Yemen

Aden

Somalia

Mogadishu

△ A victim of her own violence, a Palestinian terrorist lies dead in Mogadishu. Moreover, after the failure of the hijack, which was to have been used to secure the release of the Baader-Meinhof gang from prison, the leaders of the gang committed suicide (see page 8).

Hope for the future?

▽ With the increase in aircraft hijacking in the 1970s, airport security was tightened up considerably. Armed security guards, and even armoured cars outside airport terminals, like those in the photograph below, have become common sights. The use of these and other security measures, will make it increasingly difficult to smuggle weapons aboard aircraft, or machine gun innocent passengers at check-in desks.

As a product of modern society, terrorism is here to stay. Deterrence is expensive. Therefore, success in fighting terrorism will depend on two developments: improvements in government counter-measures, and the increased role of intelligence gathering, to help states to anticipate terrorist attacks.

In future, governments will concentrate more on the penetration of terrorist groups, using informers. They will also monitor potentially dangerous situations more closely, using information stored on computers. Society must outwit terrorists, rather than outfight them. This is our hope for the future.

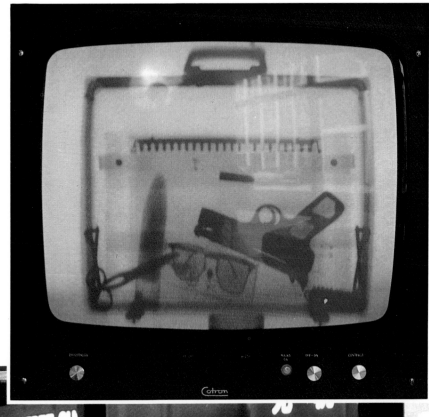

▷ To deter terrorist attacks, airports today X-ray baggage for hidden weapons.

▽ Body searches of passengers are also frequently made. However, these measures are expensive. One study found the cost of such screening in the USA, in three years alone, came to nearly $200 million.

Terrorists world-wide

Argentina
The Montoneros continue to remain Latin America's principal terrorist movement, which makes its living by kidnapping Western businessmen. It first came to prominence in 1970, by kidnapping the former President Pedro Aramburu and subjecting him to a "people's trial". Although it lost many of its members in the government's anti-terrorist campaign of the late 1970s, in which over 20,000 people perished (many of whom were innocent), it is still active.

Egypt
The Muslim Brotherhood was responsible for the assassination of President Sadat in 1982. Founded in 1928, it is a radical Islamic organisation which wishes to rid Egypt of Western influence. Occasionally it has contested elections as a political party, but for most of its history, it has been banned and forced underground.

France
Action Directe is an anarchist movement, founded in 1979, to bring down the French state. Inspired by the Red Brigade and the Red Army Faction, it has confined its attacks largely to symbols of state authority, such as magistrates courts and police stations. Its most recent attacks have been on NATO depots and installations.

India
Dal Khalsa, a militant Sikh organisation founded in 1979 to campaign for an independent Sikh homeland. It has planted a number of bombs on Air India flights, and is suspected of killing over 370 passengers on a flight from Canada. It was also responsible for the assassination of Prime Minister Indira Gandhi.

Pakistan
The Al-Zulfikar Movement emerged in 1981 to overthrow President Zia ul-Haq. It is named after the former Prime Minister Zulfikar Ali Bhutto, who was executed in 1979 after a military coup. The movement has carried out several bomb attacks, including one on Karachi National Station, as well as a number of aircraft hijacks on flights from the Middle East. It is based in Afghanistan, where it is financed by the Soviet Union.

South Africa
The African National Congress (ANC) in 1984 carried out over 40 attacks on civilian targets and on major economic targets, such as a nuclear power plant near Cape Town. Founded in 1912, it turned to violence in 1960 after all political activity by the black inhabitants of the country was prohibited. It uses terror as one tactic among many to achieve political power.

Spain
The Freedom for the Basque Homeland Movement (ETA) is, after the IRA, the most dangerous of all Western Europe's terrorist movements. In one year, 1968, it killed 350 people. Its tactics include kidnapping state officials and putting them on "trial". It conducted 60 such trials in 1978. It has also murdered high-ranking officials, especially judges. Its principal victim to date was the Spanish Prime Minister Carrero Blanco in 1973.

Sri Lanka
The Sri Lankan People's Liberation Front, founded in 1965, made the headlines in 1984 with pro-Tamil demonstrations throughout the country. It first turned to armed struggle in 1971, carrying out attacks on 90 police stations. Although it suffered a severe defeat in the mid-1970s, it has merely lain dormant and is now campaigning for an independent Tamil state.

Thailand
The Pattani United Liberation Organisation (PULO) is the most active of the country's radical Muslim groups, with over 300 members. Financed by Libya, it is not a guerilla force, but a classical terrorist movement. It has carried out arson attacks in the capital Bangkok, which in 1981 claimed the lives of 50 victims.

Chronology

1877 The *Huascar* is hijacked, making it the first ship to be seized by a terrorist group, who were from Peru.

1881 Tsar Alexander II is assassinated in Russia by a group of terrorists.

1914 The Austro-Hungarian Archduke Franz Ferdinand is assassinated by Gavrilo Princip, a member of the Black Hand terrorist organisation. This event sparks off World War I.

1937 The Geneva Convention is the first international convention on terrorism. It was triggered by the murder of King Alexander II of Yugoslavia, and the French Foreign Minister, three years before.

1954 The second convention on terrorism is held, and the proposals made have yet to be agreed to by the United Nations.

1961 The first plane hijacking to Cuba takes place.

1963 The Tokyo Air Convention is held to discuss air hijacking.

1968 The US ambassador in Guatemala is assassinated, which leads to a spate of attacks throughout the world, which claim the lives of five US ambassadors by 1980.

1970-71 First the Hague Convention and then the Montreal Convention against terrorism are held.

1972 The Israeli athletes are massacred, by Arab terrorists, at the Munich Olympics.

1974 The first embassy siege in The Hague takes place, carried out by the Japanese Red Army.

1978-79 A revolution in Iran topples the Shah, and brings to power a radical Islamic government. This government is committed to the use of terrorism to bring about Islamic revolution.

1983 The first major car bombing in Beirut takes place. Over 300 French and US servicemen die.

1985 The *Achille Lauro* is hijacked, the first major ship hijacking since 1877.

Turkey

The Grey Wolves were allegedly involved in the attempted assassination of John Paul II in 1982. Unlike most terrorist movements, it is a right-wing organisation which was founded in 1976 to engage in commando-style operations against left-wing "enemies of the state".

Yugoslavia

The Croatian Revolutionary Brotherhood has been fighting for an independent Croatian republic since 1945. It is one of the few terrorist movements to operate in a communist country. Based in Australia, it has international offices in West Germany and several other West European countries. Its principal activity has been the murder of Yugoslav diplomats, notably the ambassador to Sweden.

Index

Photographic Credits:
Cover and pages 13, 14, 16, 18, 20, 21 and back cover; Frank Spooner: pages 4/5, 11 and 24; Associated Press: pages 7, 8 and 27; Stern: pages 9, 22 and 23; Photosource/Keystone: pages 10, 12, 19 and 25; John Hillelson: page 28; Zefa: page 29 (top); IAL: page 29 (bottom); Colorific.

With many thanks to:
Control Risks Information Service Ltd

PRINTED IN BELGIUM BY

proost
INTERNATIONAL BOOK PRODUCTION